Ice Hockey Tips: Bite-Size Techniques to Boost Your Game

Ed Tennyson

Ice Hockey Tips: Bite-Size Techniques To Boost Your Game

ISBN-13: 978-1463714321

ISBN-10: 1463714327

Copyright Notice

All Rights Reserved ©2011 Ed Tennyson
First Printing: 2011.

See all of our books at: http://www.BackPocketBooks.com

You may not distribute or sell this book or modify it in any way. The editorial arrangement, analysis, and professional commentary are subject to this copyright notice. No portion of this book may be copied, retransmitted, reposted, duplicated, or otherwise used without the express written approval of the author, except by reviewers who may quote brief excerpts in connection with a review.

United States laws and regulations are public domain and not subject to copyright. Any unauthorized copying, reproduction, translation, or distribution of any part of this material without permission by the author is prohibited and against the law.

Disclaimer and Terms of Use: No information contained in this book should be considered as financial, tax, or legal advice. Your reliance upon information and content obtained by you at or through this publication is solely at your own risk. BackPocketBooks.com or the authors assume no liability or responsibility for damage or injury to you, other persons, or property arising from any use of any product, information, idea, or instruction contained in the content or services provided to you through this book. Reliance upon information contained in this material is solely at the reader's own risk. The authors have no financial interest in and receive no compensation from manufacturers of products or websites mentioned in this book.

Whilst attempts have been made to verify information provided in this publication, neither the author nor the publisher assumes any responsibilities for errors, omissions or contradictory information contained in this book. The author and publisher make no representation or warranties with respect to the accuracy, applicability, fitness, or completeness of the contents of this book. The information contained in this book is strictly for educational purposes. The author and publisher do not warrant the performance, effectiveness or applicability of any information or sites listed or linked to in this book.

All references and links are for information purposes only and are not warranted for content, accuracy or any other implied or explicit purpose. Results from using any information in this book will be totally dependent on individual circumstances and factors beyond the control of the author. The author's results may vary from your results. This book is not intended as legal, health, or diet advice.

The reader of this publication assumes all responsibility for the use of these materials and information. Some links in this document may earn the publisher a sales commission. Ed Tennyson assume no responsibility or liability whatsoever on behalf of any purchaser or reader of these materials.

PART 1

Choosing the Right Length For Your Ice Hockey Stick

Learning how to play ice hockey well begins with knowing how to choose the right ice hockey stick.

After all, you will only be able to take full advantage of all your training and practice if you have the right gear and equipment.

The wrong equipment and gear can hamper the performance of even the most well-trained hockey player.

This makes it doubly important for you to learn how to choose your hockey stick properly.

There are several factors you need to take into consideration when you are choosing a hockey stick, and the length of the stick is perhaps one of the most important of these considerations.

That's because the length of your hockey stick can affect to a large extent your ability to handle the stick, pass the puck, and shoot.

Even your skating can be affected by the length of your stick.

In general, most hockey experts say that your hockey stick should reach your chin when you have your skates on.

Of course, there are some who argue that it should be a bit longer while others say it should be shorter.

Your own preference will play a large part in the decision as to exactly how long your hockey stick should be.

Typically, however, defensive players like to have longer sticks than offensive players because it gives them better reach for poke checking.

Those who hold centre position as well as players who do a lot of stick handling typically want a shorter stick for better control in case of a face-off.

Once you have chosen your hockey stick based on other considerations such as brand, quality, and design, you can proceed with the decision of whether to lengthen, shorten, or keep it at its current length.

If you decide to lengthen your stick, you will need a wooden hockey stick butt.

This is a wooden knob that is usually 6" in length, which you insert into the end of your stick's shaft.

If adding 6" to your stick is too much, you can cut the butt to attain the desired length.

To shorten your hockey stick, simply use a hacksaw to cut it down to your desired length.

There are also some players who intentionally shorten their stick and then add a wooden butt simply because they like the solid feel that the butt provides.

You would also do well to take note that a longer stick allows you to create more flex and more power when taking a long-distance shot.

So, perhaps the best way to decide on the right length of your hockey stick is to first decide what kind of a player you are.

Once you've made this decision, you might want to experiment with varying lengths.

Practice passing, handling, skating, and shooting with sticks of different lengths to determine which length perfectly complements your style.

While there are definitely a lot of rules and trends that can help you determine the right length of ice hockey stick you should use, it ultimately boils down to your own preference.

What's important is for you to determine which length allows you to perform your game at maximum levels and then stick to that length.

Part 2
How to Determine The Right Blade Curve For Your Ice Hockey Stick

Having the right ice hockey stick can sometimes make all the difference in the world when it comes to enhancing your skills in stick handling, passing, shooting, and puck control.

To be more specific, having just the right curve on the blade of your stick can spell the difference between a passable slap shot and an amazing one.

It can also determine to a large extent whether your passes will be wobbly and rolling or flat and swishing.

It is therefore very important to make sure you have the right blade curve so you can get the most out of your passes and shots.

There are several things you need to consider when choosing the right blade curve for your style.

Take note that each ice hockey stick has several variances in toe curves, heel curves, open face, closed face, square toe, round toe, shaft to blade angle, and blade length.

All these variances will greatly affect the way the puck comes off your blade when you pass or shoot.

And each variance can be mixed and matched with any of the other variances to create even more variations.

Each manufacturer of ice hockey sticks offer you the different variations of curves and angles on the blade, and you can also expect each manufacturer to have a different name for each combination of angles and curves.

The first step you need to take in making the decision as to which blade curve is right for you is to familiarize yourself with all available options.

Once you've got all your options familiarized, take your research one step deeper and study which particular blade complements which style of passing and shooting.

There are hockey sticks with blade curves that are designed for defensive players and others that are designed for offensive players.

There are also blade curves that work best for slap shots while others are ideal for wrist shots.

After learning the advantages and disadvantages of each option, you're ready to take the next step in finding the right blade curve for your ice hockey stick.

Perhaps the best way to truly determine which blade curve is best for your style is to actually try and compare your available options.

A lot of hockey stores now have shooting areas where you can try out their products.

Take advantage of these shooting areas and try out all available sticks they have for you.

Make sure you wear skates when you test the hockey sticks because handling a hockey stick without skates is an entirely different experience than doing it with skates.

The safest and surest way to determine the blade curve best suited to your playing style is to try a slap shot, wrist shot, snap shot, pass, saucers, gong top shelf at close range, and as many other moves as you can think of with each hockey stick the store will allow you to test.

While you may find the sheer number of variations in ice hockey stick blades a bit overwhelming, always remember that finding the blade curve best suited to your specific style and personal needs is invaluable for the improvement of your game.

Once you've found the perfect blade curve, you'll find that your shot has dramatically improved and so has your passing and puck handling skills.

You might want to buy more than one so that your back-up ice hockey stick is sure to perform just as well as your main stick.

You should also remember to make a note of which blade curve you prefer so you can easily replace it when you need to.

PART 3
How to Ensure the Right Fit for Your Ice Hockey Skates

Your ice hockey skates are perhaps the most important part of your hockey equipment because your ability to move effortlessly on the ice is vital to your overall performance in the game.

Playing with ill-fitting skates can make the entire game a nightmare for you.

Aside from that, it can also increase your risk for injury.

Choosing skates that are a perfect fit should be an easy task, but the problem is that there are so many myths running around such that a lot of players end up buying skates that are completely wrong for them.

When you get a pair of ice skates, choose one that's snug but not painful.

Take note that a pair of skates are not meant to fit like a pair of shoes or slippers.

Instead, you should be able to actually feel them on your feet – against your ankles, your heels, your instep, and your toes.

If your toes feel painfully pinched, then the skates are too small, but if your feet can slide easily into them, then they're too big.

If you already have a pair of ice hockey skates and they just happen to be too small, don't fret; there's still a way to fix them.

Bring your skates to a hockey shop to have them stretched accordingly.

If, for example, the overall size of your skates is perfect, but you need to accommodate thicker ankles, then the hockey shop can use a technique that stretches out just a small area of the boots.

On the other hand, if you just happened to buy hockey skates that are too big, the only remedy is to grow into them.

Therefore, unless you're buying the skates for a child to use the following year, you have to make sure your hockey skates aren't too big.

Remember that the more room your feet have to move around in your boots, the more likely you are to develop blisters or bone spurs.

Remember that your toes should touch the front of your boots.

Test the fit of your skates by standing on both feet with your skates laced up.

If your toes touch the front of the boots, then you have a perfect fit.

You should also kick your heels against the floor once or twice to make sure they're settled all the way back in the skate.

Another important consideration in determining the right fit of hockey skates is the length of the insoles.

An excellent way to ensure that your skates' insoles are of the right length is to remove them, place them flat on the floor, and then stand on them.

If you're an adult player, then your toes and heels should come right to the edge of the insoles.

For children, the toes and heels should come within a finger's width from the edge to give room for growth.

In the same way, you should ensure the right fit when choosing a pair of hockey inline skates, which has to fit snugly in order to keep your feet from wobbling when you skate.

You would do well to find a full-service pro hockey shop, as they can help you get the perfect fit and provide you with some useful advice on other hockey equipment, including hockey sticks and goalie equipment.

Part 4
Fundamentals of Ice Hockey

Any aspiring hockey player should definitely master the fundamental skills before even thinking about learning any special techniques or tricks of the trade.

As with any other sport, the best hockey players are those who have mastered the fundamentals such that it has become second nature to them.

Skating, passing, and shooting are the most important basic hockey skills you need to learn.

Take note that just because they're basic skills, it doesn't necessarily mean they're easy to master.

Skating is perhaps the single most important hockey skill.

If you want to be able to excel in the sport, then you'll need to be able to skate really well.

Skating, in itself, is something many people find a bit difficult to learn, and the difficulty is compounded by the fact that you'll have to skate on ice, which is a very slippery surface.

Another problem most people face when trying to learn how to ice skate is that it can be quite difficult to find a skating rink and you'll most likely have to pay for your time on the rink.

It's important that you make the most of your time on the ice.

As soon as you master one skating skill, move on immediately to another.

Focusing too much on a skill you're already good at can lead to stagnation in your overall development.

Instead, you should place more focus on a skating move at which you find yourself struggling.

This way, you can become adept at all the essential skating moves, which include tight turns, hockey stops, forward stride, crossovers, backward skating, and edge control.

Passing often comes a bit more naturally for most hockey players than skating does.

It's best to apply the same concept you use in mastering your skating skills when you work on your passing skills.

Remember that practice makes perfect, so don't ever think that you're wasting time when you're doing passing drills.

An excellent way to enhance your passing skills is to practice sailing the puck instead of whacking at it.

A pass works better when the puck simply slides on the ice rather than bounces to your teammate.

Whacking is only a good idea for powerfully shooting the puck towards the goal.

Shooting is obviously just as important.

After all, you can't possibly score goals unless you can successfully shoot the puck.

A good shot can change the tempo of a game, and it can change the player as well.

There's no better way to boost your confidence than to make a good shot, right?

This is the reason why most coaches have basically the same philosophy when it comes to their team's offense, which is for players to get the puck to the net.

More than just getting the puck to the net, however, you should strive to pick the corners and perfectly hit the spots where the goalie is not.

Think about it:

Getting the puck to the net is easy enough, but the problem is that the net is almost always guarded by the goalie.

The corners, on the other hand, are almost always open, although they're much more difficult to hit.

When practicing your shooting skills, be sure to work on your wrist shot, snap shot, slap shot, and backhand shot.

You should also work on quick release, shooting hard, and shooting for corners.

Of course, there are several other skills you need to learn as a hockey player.

But skating, passing, and shooting are the most important fundamental skills you need to master.

Once you become adept at these skills, it'll be so much easier to learn other techniques and tricks.

PART 5
Hockey Tricks Every Beginner Should Learn

As a beginner in the sport of hockey, you need to master ice skating and stick handling, among other skills.

Understandably, mastering these skills can take years of hard work.

The good news is that you can bring your game to the next level while you're still trying to master the fundamental skills by learning a few tricks of the trade.

These tricks are minor skills that can easily add more flare to your game.

Running Onto the Ice

As you come out of the locker room, do a little run on the walkway, jump onto the ice and then immediately start skating as you land.

Aside from giving you a grand entrance, this also demonstrates that you have excellent balance and a good understanding of skating.

You just might succeed at intimidating your opponents a little.

Jumping Over the Boards

When teams change lines in hockey, remember that the open door is reserved for the players coming off the ice.

If you're coming onto the ice, then you should be standing by the boards, ready to jump over them and start skating to position as soon as you're called.

You have the option of straddling the boards, but jumping over them is so much more dramatic and can effectively pump you up for a good game.

Picking up a Puck

When the game stops and you're near the puck, it's a good idea to pick it up with your hand and then toss it to the nearest referee.

This little action is an excellent way of demonstrating your balance.

And as your skills grow, you can move on to picking the puck up with your stick, but for now, the hand pick-up is a smooth move that'll help you improve both your balance and flexibility.

Popping up After a Fall

As a beginner in the sport, you should expect to fall down several times.

Therefore, it's important for you to practice getting up from a fall as quickly as you can.

When you observe hockey professionals, you'll notice that they seem to pop up on both feet after taking a fall.

You, too, can master the art of popping up.

Practice this move by skating forward with your shin guards on and then dropping to your knees.

Now, try to pop up and then skate at your fastest speed.

Work on this drill until you can successfully pop up each time you fall.

Dribbling the Puck with Your Feet

It can be quite difficult for a beginner to manipulate the puck with the hockey stick, so you might want to try bouncing it on your skates for starters.

During practice or warm-ups, try to trap the puck as a soccer player traps the ball.

As soon as the puck is at your feet, try to kick it to your skate blade.

This is a good trick to use when you're battling against the boards, where it can be a lot easier to just kick the puck into open space.

Remember that every sport has its own set of tricks, and hockey is no exception.

Every beginner should make use of at least a few of these tricks to make it a bit easier to transition from being a novice to a hockey veteran.

PART 6
How to Skate Faster

As a beginner in the sport of hockey, learning to skate well is probably the easiest and surest way to make you enjoy the game even more than you do.

Aside from increasing your enjoyment of the game, mastering skating skills is also very helpful to your overall game.

Whether you're in an odd-man rush or rushing past a defensive player on a breakaway, your skating skills will allow you to live up to hockey's slogan of being the fastest game on ice.

In order to skate faster on ice, you'll have to take three key factors into consideration.

The first is the act of putting your weight on the skates.

The second is maximizing your edges, and the third is learning how to stop effectively.

The same principles are basically followed whether you're skating forwards or backwards, except for when you're pushing the puck.

Putting your weight on the skates simply means you have to make sure that every push of your skate places as much of your body weight as possible over the blade.

This key element works hand-in-hand with maximizing your edges, which requires your body weight to push off against a strongly-angled edge.

For example, if you're pushing off of your right skate, then the inside right skate edge should be positioned at a 45-degree angle.

This allows you to push hard with your right leg and skate forward driving your left leg.

As your knee begins to straighten out from a hard push, make sure your left leg begins to angle itself to a 45-degree angle, so it can pick up the pace and you can push off with your left leg as soon as your right leg exhausts its push.

You may then bring your right leg up past your left leg and plant it on the ice such that it can glide easily and be prepared when it comes time to push off with your right leg again.

A key point you need to bear in mind is that you should be very sensitive to every single aspect of your skating stride.

As a beginner, you're not likely to be given too many opportunities for personal coaching, so you have to make sure that you're sensitive to how fast you're going.

And when you play in scrimmages or go ice skating at public rinks, try to identify people with good stride and don't hesitate to ask them for tips.

You should also take note that most people who don't skate fast are also the ones who don't know how to stop correctly.

In fact, their lack of ability in stopping is perhaps the very reason why they avoid skating fast in the first place.

The key to a good hockey stop is learning how to pick up your feet and angle them into the ice.

You can start building up this skill by practicing a "snow plow" stop and then gradually moving on to plowing with just one foot.

Lastly, a very good way of ensuring that you're able to skate fast for hockey is to always keep your skate blades sharp.

Sharp edges allow for stronger strides and more forceful stops.

If you feel that your stride is slipping, then it may be time to sharpen your skates.

PART 7
Ice Hockey Skating Drills

Other than scoring, skating is definitely the most important aspect of ice hockey.

After all, you can't expect to become a good hockey player unless you know how to skate really well.

Ice hockey skating drills are therefore necessary for anyone wanting to get into the game of ice hockey.

These drills are sure to help you bring your skating skills to optimum levels and give you a better chance of becoming a great hockey player.

Power Start Drill

Being able to skate with a fast and powerful start is often a big advantage in a game of ice hockey, and this drill helps you develop just that skill.

The aim of this drill is to have one player pull another right up to the red line.

The player being pulled should hold on to the other player's jersey and then the one in the lead should take several strides until he comes to a gliding stop at the red line.

After 5-6 pulls, the players should switch places.

4-Minute Skating Drill

This drill helps you become more comfortable with the act of skating and helps increase your skating speed.

The team is divided into groups of three players.

The first player in each group will then skate from the blue line to the middle red line and then back again at full speed.

The next players do the same, and the drill goes on for four minutes.

Piranha Pivot

This drill promotes flexibility and can be practiced even when you're alone.

Beginning at one end of the rink, you should skate at full speed to the blue line, pivot and then skate backwards to the second blue line where you pivot once again and skate to the red line.

You should then go behind the net, pivot and skate backwards to the blue line, pivot again and continue skating until you reach the point where you started.

4-Stop Drill

Just as it is important to develop your skill in starting quickly and powerfully, it's also important for you to know how to stop properly.

With this drill, the players will be asked to line up at one end of the rink.

The first player then moves clockwise, skating to each of the four face-off marks.

Each time the player reaches a mark he should power stop, look up, and wave to the coach.

And when all four marks have been hit, the player then skates to the back of the line as the second player takes off to do the drill.

The drill is repeated 4-5 times without breaks.

Chasing the Wind

This drill is a good cardio exercise that also helps improve your starting and stopping skills.

The players are made to line up on the blue line.

When the coach blows the whistle, all players should skate to the second blue line and then stop.

Again, the coach will blow the whistle, at which point the players should skate to the red line.

The coach will then blow the whistle again and the players to the starting line.

The coach will then make the players go faster by decreasing the stop time at each line for the succeeding repetitions.

Practicing ice hockey skating drills are indeed advisable for both beginners and advanced hockey players.

You should never forget the fact that you can't reach the net and score a goal unless you first know how to skate.

And you can hardly become a good hockey player unless you know how to skate really well.

PART 8
Basic Rules of Pinching

If you want to play better defense in ice hockey, then you should definitely strive to become the most reliable defensive player on the ice.

Perhaps the most common problem that besets defensive hockey players is the question of when exactly is the right time to pinch.

Many players hesitate to pinch for fear of being too early or too late.

As a result, they often fail to take advantage of a possibly excellent defensive play.

To put it simply, pinching is the act of rushing forward off of your opponent's blue line when you team is in the opponent's zone.

What makes this simple move more complicated is the decision you have to make as to when exactly you should pinch.

If you achieve the perfect timing, then you'll be giving your team an immediate advantage and ensure that your team keeps possession of the puck.

But, if you're timing is bad, then your opponent can easily have two to three men rushing back at you, and you lose the advantage.

When to Pinch

The perfect time to pinch will depend on the exact game situation you find yourself in, and with enough experience you'll be better able to read the game and the decision of whether to pinch or not will become instinctive.

For starters, though, you'd do well to follow some simple guidelines that'll help you pinch when the right opportunity presents itself.

One of the best opportunities to pinch is when the person you're pinching towards doesn't have the puck yet or when he doesn't have full control of the puck yet.

This is the perfect opportunity for you to take time and space away from your opponent, so do it.

The kind of relationship you have with your defensive partner can also affect your pinching skills to a large extent.

The more comfortable you are with your partner, the more confident you'll be at pinching, knowing your partner is always there to cover you when necessary.

Be sure to talk to your partner before and after each game to discuss game situations and strategies.

You should also take note of the composition of the other team when you decide to pinch.

If your opponent has their first line on the ice, you should be more cautious when you pinch.

When Not to Pinch

In general, you should avoid pinching if your defensive partner is not yet a very reliable defense player.

You should also refrain from pinching if your teammates are out of position, particularly your wingers.

Being out of position keeps them from being able to cover you.

And if you're playing against an exceptionally fast winger, you be very cautious in your game, or you just might get burned.

The score is also an important consideration when deciding whether to pinch or not.

It's advisable not to pinch if the score is tied or if you're leading by a goal or two.

In these stations, your main responsibility is to shut the other team down, and you're expected to play a more conservative game.

Mistakes at this point can be very costly, so you should remember to defend first and attack only when absolutely necessary.

On the other hand, if your team is down by a goal or two, then you should pinch when the opportunity presents itself because that might be just what your team needs.

Pinching is something that can be very useful and may even spell the difference between a loss and a win in certain game situations.

As long as you follow the basic rules of when to pinch and when to hold back on a pinch, then you should be able to work effectively towards becoming more comfortable with this move.

Soon, pinching will become instinctive and the decision of whether to pinch or not will come more easily to you.

PART 9
How to Become an Effective Goalie

If your dream is to become a goalie in the game of ice hockey, then you'll have to learn how to be effective in this position.

Generally, you must have good reflexes, fast hands, and most of all, good eyesight.

You should also possess a good deal of courage because the puck can come directly at you at amazing speeds.

Add to that the fact that you are the last man between your opponents and the net, and being a goalie can indeed be more than a little intimidating, which is why courage is a very important attribute of a good goalie.

Apart from courage, confidence is also something a goalie should have.

You need to believe you are the best in your field.

This kind of positive thinking is especially useful when your team is having a bad game, as it helps keep your spirits up and keeps you focused on your responsibilities as a goalie.

No matter how good you are, there will be times when you'll have a bad game, but even then, you'll have to keep on believing in your abilities as well as those of your teammates.

And you might think that skating isn't as important to a goalie as it is to the other players in the team.

On the contrary, your skating skills can have a huge impact on how good you are in goaltending.

As a goalie, you not only have to be a good skater, but you also have to be able to skate backwards at top speed.

Be sure to practice skating with your goal pads and other goaltending equipment on because that's how you're going to skate in an actual game.

When you're tending goal, you should remember to always keep your eyes on the puck.

This is, in fact, one of the most important rules in goaltending.

Let your teammates worry about the other aspects of the game.

Your job is to watch the puck and prevent it from getting past you into the net.

Considering this, you should also try to stay at or very near the net.

Goalies generally don't have any business going around the ring trying to clear the puck; that's a job for your defensive players.

Another important rule you should bear in mind is to stay on your feet as much as possible.

Understandably, you'll have a better chance of blocking shots and getting rebounds when you're on your feet than when you're sprawled on the ice.

Of course, there may be times when you'll absolutely need to go down to stop a puck.

When you do, make sure that you fall in such a way that you're ready to bounce right back up to your feet.

One of the surest ways to stop a puck from entering the net is to catch it, so you'll definitely need to learn how to use your hands.

Using your hands properly allows you to ensure that the puck doesn't rebound off your gear and into the net.

As soon as you catch the puck, you should toss it into the corner for your teammates to get it out of your end of the rink.

A good way to improving your skills at catching the puck is to ask your team's best hitter to fire 30-40 consecutive shots your way during practice and you'll try to stop the shots using only your hands.

Above all, you should remember that being a goalie can be very strenuous, which makes it doubly important for you to be in top physical condition.

You should a healthy diet and get plenty of rest between games and practices.

You should also exercise and do your drills regularly.

Finally, never try to copy any other goalie's style.

Instead, you should find a style you're most comfortable with and stick to that.

PART 10
Tips for Becoming A Butterfly Style Goalie

The most popular goaltending style these days is known as butterfly style.

What's god about this style is that it allows you to cover the bottom part of the net really well and also provides for easy lateral movement across the crease.

This may be why both amateurs and professionals are now using butterfly style goaltending more than ever.

A goalie goes into the butterfly position by pushing his knees forward and then dropping onto the ice.

When you decide to do this, take note that you should continue to maintain your balance and stay in control of your game.

You should also strive to maintain an upright position at all times so you can cover more net and always keep the puck in sight.

Your glove and blocker should be in front of your body at shoulder height, and your stick should be held at an angle.

If a shot comes at you from close range, press your glove and blocker against your side, ensuring there are no gaps at your armpits.

While butterfly style goaltending involves getting down on your knees, it doesn't mean you'll have to stay down all the time.

In fact, you should avoid staying down as much as possible.

This style is used primarily to stop low to mid shots and you should only get into butterfly position once the shot has been made, not when the puck is still moving around or outside your zone.

The exception is when the puck is in the crease or is very close in the slot.

Perhaps the biggest mistake a lot of goalies make is staying focused on the shooter instead of the puck.

Your body should always face the puck and your eyes should be glued to it at all times.

If you watch the shooter, he might be able to trick you into moving away from the puck, thus scoring a point against you.

So, remember to always follow the puck and not the shooter.

Another important rule you need to remember is to always play at the top of your crease because this reduces the amount of space that a shooter will be able to shoot at.

It is especially important for you to follow this rule if you are a smaller goalie because playing at the top of your crease makes you bigger at the net.

Finally, you should always make sure that you're in the best position to make the save.

This means you should always be square to the puck and that you don't cheat to either side.

Being off your angle even the slightest bit gives the shooter a bit more room to shoot at.

Whenever it's safe to do so, you should check behind you to ensure that you're still in a good angle for the save.

Butterfly style goaltending can indeed be very effective both for the beginner and the experienced goalie.

But, you'll have to do it properly, of course, in order to make full use of its benefits and advantages.

Following the basic rules of butterfly goaltending will surely bring you on the road to stardom as an ice hockey goalie.

PART 11
How to Become a Better Hockey Player

Imagine that a hockey team is a chain.

Each player is symbolized by one of the interconnected links in the chain.

Now, if one of these links is broken, the entire link is in danger of falling.

In the same way, the success of an entire hockey team depends largely on the performance of each player on the team.

If one team member doesn't work as hard as the others and falls behind in skills development as a result, the performance of the entire team in a game could be affected.

You now know how important it is to enhance your craft as a hockey player.

Surely, you wouldn't want to be the weak link in your team, would you?

Remember that knowledge is the most important thing you have to equip yourself with if you want to improve your hockey skills.

Knowledge refers to the technical matters and techniques you need to learn when playing hockey.

These things also help you learn how to anticipate your opponent's moves during a game.

And of course, you'll need to learn the basic rules governing the game so you'll know exactly what you can and cannot do.

Training and development are also very important in becoming a good hockey player.

When you already know the rules of the game and you've learned some of the best techniques, you'll have to develop your skills.

This way, you'll not only play good defense by anticipating your opponent's moves, but you'll be able to play better offense as well.

Now, you'll have to remember that team practice isn't enough to develop your hockey skills; you'll have to take the time to practice by yourself as well.

Remember as well that becoming a better hockey player requires discipline and perseverance.

Whatever your performance is in a particular game, you should always challenge yourself to do better the next time.

But, you shouldn't get discouraged if you fail to take your game one step higher from one game to the next.

What's important is that you give each game your all.

Sooner or later you will succeed in playing better than you did in your previous game and when that happens, you'll be pleased to see yourself grow as a player.

Another thing you need to take into consideration when working to become a better hockey player is your physical condition.

Remember that hockey is a tough game, both physically and mentally.

The physical aspect of the game is particularly taxing, as you're likely to get knocked around for the most part.

If you win the game, then you may not actually mind the physical beating, but if you lose, the pain and exhaustion you feel may double.

This is why it's important to be in good physical and mental condition when you get into this game.

When you watch a hockey game, you would surely understand the need for physical conditioning.

Players get knocked around and might even get hit by the puck in the course of the game.

Regularly doing intense workouts is probably the best way to get into the right shape for ice hockey.

And always remember to take care of your body not just during a game, but also before and after one.

As regards mental conditioning, this is achieved differently from one person to the next.

What's important is that you have fun and that you focus on your specific role as a player.

If you win, then by all means celebrate that win.

But, if you lose, don't take the loss too hard.

Instead, take it as a challenge and strive to play better on your next game.

PART 12
How to Develop a Successful Power Play

In any hockey game, having a dominant power play can spell the difference between a win and a loss for your team.

And one of the most important ways of leading towards a power play is to win the face-off.

Remember that you get into a face-off in the offensive zone of the opposing team.

Therefore, getting the puck back to your teammate allows your team to set up properly for a power play; otherwise, your opponent may clear the puck out of the zone and you'll be wasting precious time.

Setting up into attack formation is the next big step towards an effective power play.

As soon as you get the puck, each player should proceed to their designated area so your power play can proceed with ease.

Being able to execute these movements perfectly creates space for your team and gives you plenty of opportunities to score.

Puck movement is also something your team needs to master if you want to develop an effective power play.

This is the best way for you to keep the opposing penalty killers running around, thus eventually wearing them out.

The ability to move the puck around also gives you more time to make better decisions as to the right play to execute in specific game situations.

And when you tire the penalty killers out, the defense will inevitably leave an opening for you to make the shot.

Quite understandably, getting a shot into the net is crucial to a successful power play.

After all, your efforts in executing a power play will all be for naught unless you can get that shot into the net.

Missing a shot could result in the opponent clearing the puck and setting up for their own power play.

Remember that your opponents will try to block every single shot you make, so your ability to fake shots and move the puck is really very helpful.

When a shooter gets ready to shoot the puck into the net, it can be very useful to have other players within the shooting area.

Specifically, it's a good idea to have one player right in front of the goalie.

This player will interfere with the goalie's vision and make it more difficult for him to make a save.

And more than just the screen, the player in front of the goalie has the all-important role of getting the possible rebound and ensuring that the puck goes to the back of the net.

When there's a loose puck on the ice, take note that penalty killers are probably the hardest working and most tenacious players and they will do everything to clear that puck down the ice and kill some time.

To execute a good power play, your team should out-man the opposing team in the corners and win the battle for the loose puck.

Finally, you may have already prepared several manoeuvres to make your power play work, but unless you're able to capitalize on every opportunity you get to use those manoeuvres, you still won't be able to take full advantage of your power play.

Even if you don't score, you can still gain momentum by recognizing and utilizing scoring opportunities.

NOTES

NOTES

Printed in Great Britain
by Amazon